Dream
Symbols

Dream Symbols

by Sara Phillips

AN IMPRINT OF RUNNING PRESS
PHILADELPHIA • LONDON

9   8   7   6   5   4   3   2   1
Digit on the right indicates the number of this printing

Library of Congress Cataloging-in-Publication Number 2002100730

ISBN 0-7624-1394-8

Text written by Sara Phillips
Introduction written by Stephanie Spitler
Edited by Sara Phillips
Cover and interior design by Corinda Cook
Photos researched by Susan Oyama
Typography: Avenir, Poppl Residenz, and Stempel Schneidler

This book may be ordered by mail from the publisher.
But try your bookstore first!

Published by Courage Books, an imprint of
Running Press Book Publishers
125 South Twenty-second Street
Philadelphia, Pennsylvania 19103-4399

Visit us on the web!
www.runningpress.com

Contents

"The dream is a little hidden door in the innermost and most secret recesses of the soul, opening into that cosmic night . . ."

—Carl Jung

Unlock the door to your hidden desires and fears using the key symbols in your dreams. By gaining a better understanding of what these symbols mean, you will more fully understand what your subconscious is trying to tell you when you close your eyes at night.

As long as humans have been on the Earth, we have been dreamers. And our dreams play a major role in how we live and understand our lives. In ancient Greece, the faithful sought interpretations of their dreams from the Oracle at Delphi. In Native American Indian tribes, the esteemed position of medicine man was held by the most vivid dreamer. The ancient Romans believed that the gods revealed their wishes in the dreams of men, so interpreting those dreams became of divine importance. From premonitions to superstitions, men and women have always attempted to make sense of their dreams.

Two of the twentieth century's most important psychological minds, Sigmund Freud and Carl Jung, developed individual theories regarding the meaning of dreams. According to Freud, dreams were a combination of primal urges and our earliest recollections and impulses. However, Jung believed that dreams were manifestations of the phases we go through in life. He believed that dreams employed symbols to represent feelings or fears that we were not dealing with in our waking life. According to Jung, the subconscious acts as teacher, leading us in the direction of the most growth.

Incorporating facets of both theories, *Dream Symbols* offers interpretations for sixty of the most common dream symbols. The explanations are joined with full-color illustrations to simulate the richness of a vivid dream. In addition to the general interpretation of the symbol, questions are offered that will personalize your analysis by taking into account specific details of your dream. For example, dreaming of an apple could signify sin and temptation, or it could represent knowledge. But when you consider things like the condition of the apple or its color, the meaning changes.

Understanding what your dreams are trying to tell you is the first step to better understanding yourself and improving your life. So take a deep breath, close your eyes, and drift away, ready to decipher the language of your dreams.

Airplane

Dreams that involve travel relate to your life journey. Often, planes appear in dreams before an anticipated transition, such as moving across the country or starting a new job. If you aren't expecting anything new or different, they may indicate a strong desire for such change. If you are piloting the plane, consider your cargo: what you are carrying is the thing or person you care most deeply about. A crash symbolizes loss of power in making big decisions, and flight delays indicate frustration at not being able to move out of your current life situation.

See *bicycle, car, road.*

Angel

Angels are divine messengers and helpers, beings of light and mercy. If an angel speaks

to you in a dream, listen carefully to the message—it could carry great spiritual import,

or give you a direct line to your usually-hidden unconscious. If you ask an angel for

help, or are helped by an angel, the dream is most likely wish-fulfillment.

Apple

In western tradition, the apple symbolizes sin and temptation; it can also represent knowledge. Recall where the apple came from in the dream: if it was offered to you, perhaps someone is tempting you with worldly pleasures. The state of the apple is also important: a rotting apple means love is going sour; a golden apple means you are acquiring knowledge. If you plant apple seeds, you desire to impart knowledge to others or start a family.

See *tree.*

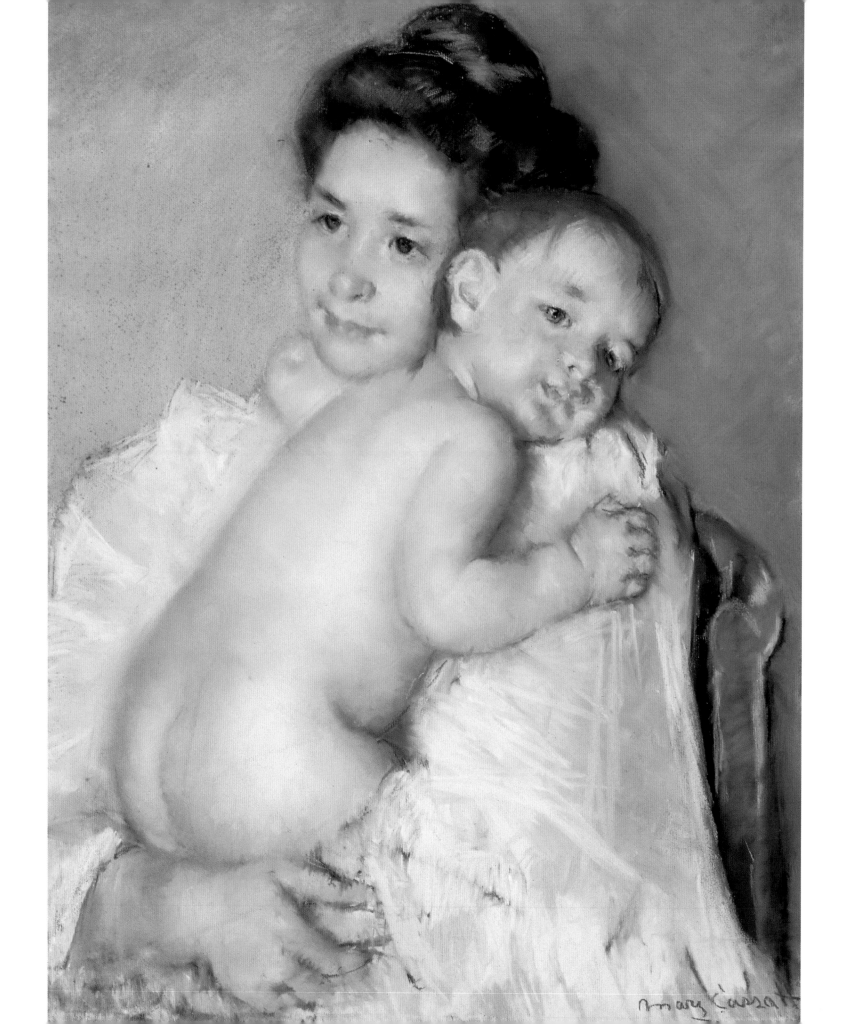

A baby is a sign of innocence, new beginning, and personal creativity. To dream you are taking care

of a newborn infers a feeling of responsibility in a particular area of your life. Perhaps you are

starting a project that will require commitment and patience. If you are the infant, you struggle with

needs that are not being met, or feel vulnerable to forces beyond your control. According to Jung,

dreams of pregnancy are signs you are entering a new stage of psychological or spiritual development.

See *child*.

Bear

A very personal symbol, the bear represents fear buried deep within the psyche. For Freudians, wild animals represent our darker impulses and hidden motives: the bear, only aggressive when provoked, can be a sign of latent rage. Black bears stand for repressed emotions and unfulfilled dreams. In an age in which humans are distanced from the natural world, it also carries cultural meaning: the bear represents a threat from the outside that is widely unknown and very powerful.

Bed

The bed is a place of comfort and rest, of infant-like vulnerability. It is the place we go to renew ourselves; for Freud, it is a symbol of the womb. The bed also acts as a sign for sexuality; it is private space another enters at your consent. If you dream someone is sleeping in your bed, your personal security is being threatened. If you dream of lying in bed, or "fall asleep" in the course of a dream sequence, you are comfortable crossing the bridge between your conscious and unconscious, and lucid dreaming is within your grasp. See *sleeping*.

Bicycle

Like most dreams involving transportation, cycling relates to your life journey. A symbol of independence gained early in life, the bicycle harkens to a younger you; perhaps ties to home have not been fully broken. To ride a bicycle successfully requires balance. If your ride is unsteady, you are struggling to find your place at work or home. If your pedals, brakes, or handlebars are oversensitive, control is the issue. For example, failed brakes are a sign that your life feels out of control, and touchy steering means the decisions you make have a wider impact than you intend.

See *airplane, car, road*.

Georges Duchesne

Blindness

Dreaming you cannot see is traditionally associated with losing the line of communication with your unconscious self. If you are suddenly blinded, consider the cause. Difficulties in sight for which there is no apparent reason indicate concern that you will not be able to perform everyday tasks, or even that you would rather not be responsible for duties that have been handed to you. "Blind spots" may also be the result of deliberate disregard of an emotional or physical problem.

Dreams about the body indicate a concern with personal image, especially the perceptions we or others have of ourselves. If any part of the body—mouth, ears, hands—is accentuated, you may be self-conscious about it, or have concerns about its disruptive potential. For instance, dreaming your ears have grown huge suggests a fear of hearing something not meant for you to know. Jung believed the right side of the body is related to the conscious, the left to the unconscious. If a region of your body is in pain, you may want to visit a doctor—your unconscious may be telling you of an actual physical problem.

See *hair, skeleton.*

Book

Books are sources of knowledge and learning, a sign of wisdom

acquired with age. If you compose a story during a dream, you are

using your subconscious as a creative outlet. Perhaps you have

less ambition or confidence in your creative pursuits when awake,

and would benefit if given more opportunity to exercise your

imagination. Books also stand as a record of the past, and may

stand for your own memory or the collective memory of your

culture. This is especially true if you are reading history or a news

item. Difficulty reading means you need to pay more attention

to your studies, or become more aware of the world around you.

Bridge

A bridge is a metaphor for a relationship between two things, and in dreams often symbolizes transition. Perhaps you are crossing from one part of your life into another, or from one psychological or emotional state into a new one. Often in dreams, passing over a bridge indicates that you are ready to move on in your life path; consider what you are leaving behind. If you are building a bridge, you are preparing for such a transition. Bridges in dreams do give you an opportunity to enact change, but may be related to anxiety, as risk is involved in making any major decision. Your feelings towards the bridge may be significant in your personal understanding of the symbol.

Candle

A lit candle is a sign of hope; an unlit candle, a sign of rejection. If a person enters your dream holding a candle, he is she will reveal something important; follow with full trust and you will find the deeper meaning. If you see a candle burning at both ends, you are using all of your reserve, and in danger of burnout. Candles on a cake point to anxiety about age, as does a wick burning down or flickering out.

See *fire*.

Car

The car represents a person's ego, the conscious, decision-making part of the self. Dreams of driving reflect upon how your unconscious views your direction in life. If you are involved in an accident or get caught speeding, your unconscious is trying to warn you to be more careful or to slow down. Consider the driver: whoever sits behind the wheel has ultimate control over your decisions. Other important factors include the road you are driving on, the state of your vehicle, and where you are driving.

See *airplane, bicycle, road.*

Cat

The domestic cat comes and goes as it pleases, relying on its caretakers as it wishes, but free to tramp into the wild at its leisure. In dreams, that cat is a sign of independence, agility, and emotional aloofness. Often, a dream of this type is a reflection on emotional distance; perhaps someone you are close to is constantly changing the level of emotional vulnerability in the relationship, or prefers to rely on his or her own internal schedule, without realizing the implications on you. Cats also symbolize sexuality.

Chess

Chess is an intellectual pursuit, a game for which strategy and experience play a large part in determining the outcome. If you dream of playing chess, you may be dealing with a situation that requires complex problem solving skills. In order to play chess, you must know the rules of the game. If you are unsure of these, you fear your lack of experience may put you at a disadvantage. If your opponent lacks the necessary skills, you are unchallenged in a specific area. Consider your adversary; if rivalry exists between you in waking life, perhaps the dream will give you an opportunity to learn more about his or her strengths or weaknesses, as well as your own.

Child

A child is a symbol of innocence, simplicity, and possibility. If you dream of being a child again, you desire to return to a place of less responsibility, or wish you could change a formative aspect of yourself. If you are taking care of a child you do not know, you are beginning a project that will require commitment and time, or are expressing parental instincts. See *baby*.

Clown

The clown is a symbol of childhood amusement, and is also associated with fear of the unknown. If you dream of a clown as an adult, you may be visiting childhood memories, or confronting something you have been afraid of since you were young. Clowns make fun of the ludicrous by being ridiculous themselves; consider the clown's message carefully, and the context in which it is made. If the clown appears in an everyday setting, you are being forced to confront an unreasonable person.

Colors

Most people dream in color, though in dreams the hues are often muted. In lucid or controlled dreaming, color is reported to be vibrant, even more "real" than in waking life. Colors in dreams often carry cultural significance, though they may have special significance for the individual dreamer as well. For instance, black is believed to betoken the unknown, signal depression, or uncover hidden sexual desires. Blue connotes optimism and communication; green is the color of money, jealousy, and new life; red signals anger and passion; and white stands for purity and wholeness.

A crown is a sign of power, political status, or wealth. As a circular object, it stands for completion, wholeness, and unity. Because crowns are only used at very formal royal ceremonies today, and not as an everyday sign of a monarch, they may function as an archetype of the recognized ruler, or the archetypal father. See *father, jewelry, old man, old woman*.

Death

Death is a sign of finality, closure, and completion.

If you dream of your own death, you are antici-

pating the end of a period of your life; it also

may indicate a need to leave the past behind. If

someone you know dies, you fear their loss, or are

struggling to break free from an intense relation-

ship. Burying something means you are leaving

behind what you no longer have need of.

Devil

Culturally, the devil is taboo. If he is helping you in a dream, perhaps you are

engaging in behavior that would be considered immoral by the outside world.

You may even desire to play out your darker desires and are using the dream-

scape as a forum for experimentation. According to Jung, evil beings represent

the destructive part of our selves, the archetypal "shadow" who acts as the

negative side of the ego. Conversely, you may have a deep fear of evil.

See *snake*.

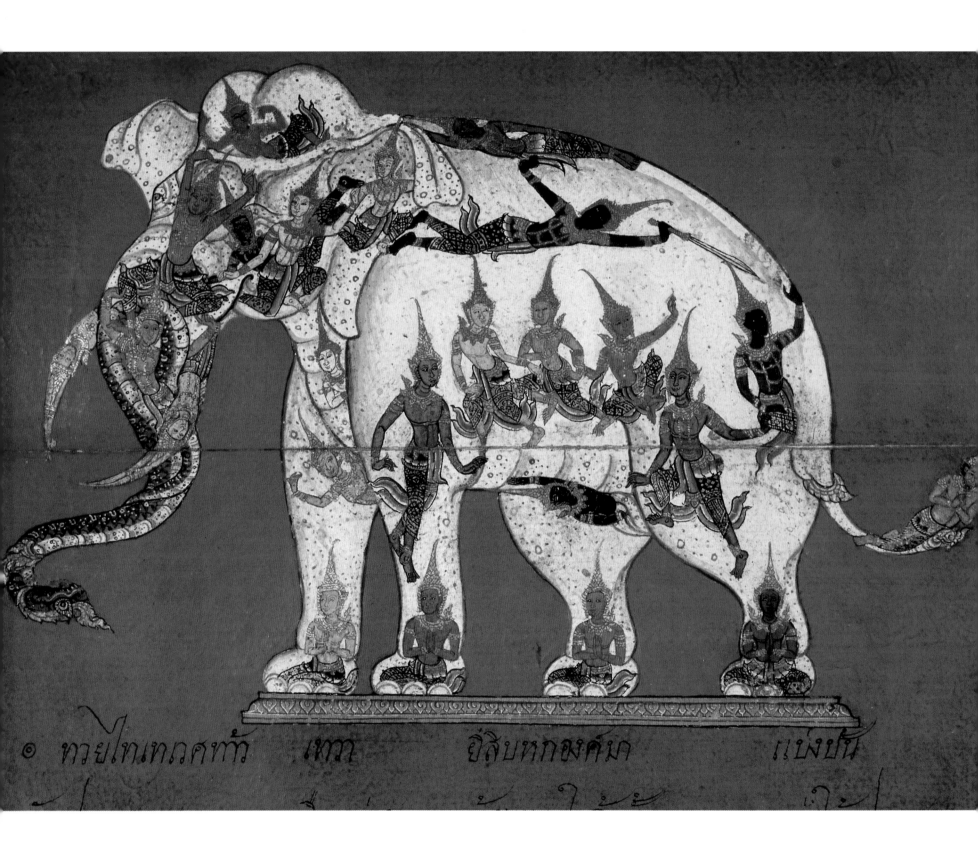

๏ ทายไทเทภศท้า   เทา   ยี่สิบหกองค์มา   แบ่งปัน

Elephant

Dreaming of an elephant may mean you are trying to remember something important, or fear your memory is faulty. The elephant is a creature of slow elegance, associated with strength and determination. Consider its purpose in the dream. If it is carrying a heavy burden, you have a task in front of you that requires outside help. If it is part of the circus, or is roaming in the jungle, consider the setting carefully; it carries cultural significance. The elephant's thick skin may be a sign that you need to take things less personally.

Father

The father is the symbol of outward authority, of practical nurture, and reason. Father-figures are often very personal in meaning. If you dream of your own father, you may be confronting issues in your past, or are dealing with authority figures. Dreaming you are in a paternal role may mean you desire to have children, or wish to impart practical wisdom to someone of lesser experience. The father may also symbolize the archetype of the wise old man.

See *old man, old woman*.

Fire

Both life-sustaining and deadly, the meaning for fire is two-sided. As a source of light and heat, it represents spiritual enlightenment. If a fire is keeping you warm, you are being nurtured. If you are in danger of being burned, this symbol may indicate fear. Fire can also act as a warning about a situation that may get out of control if not closely monitored. Fire also stands for spiritual transformation, purification, and cleansing. Like the phoenix who rises from the ashes, the dreamer may go through the flames to achieve a new spiritual or emotional state.

See *candle*.

Flying

Dreams in which you experience the ability to fly are very common; they represent a desire to lose the restrictions imposed upon you by the natural world. Flying is traditionally associated with lucid dreaming, in which the dreamer controls the course of events. Often, the dreamer needs something to aid flight, like rocket shoes, a harness, or a magic wand. If you experience difficulty while flying in a dream, ask yourself what is holding you back: this is the symbol which carries the most significance.

Food is a symbol of sustenance or waste, depending upon how it appears

in the dream. Rotting food is a sign of waste and gluttony; fresh food

symbolizes nourishment, goodness, and satisfaction. Food often carries

very personal meaning, based upon your relationship to it. For instance,

if you struggle to maintain your weight, food may represent temptation

or act as a symbol for the restrictions placed upon you when dieting.

For gourmands, food may represent renewal or satisfaction.

Gift

A gift is a symbol of the relationship between yourself and another person, and acts as a key to unlocking the feelings and expectations surrounding your friendship. If it is given without expectation of return, a gift speaks of grace. If you dream of giving disproportionate gifts, for instance, a book for a diamond ring, you are concerned that one person is more invested than the other. Consider who is giving and who is getting, and whether the gift itself bears special significance. The wrapping may also be important.

Grapes

Like most fruit, grapes are a sexual symbol. To see a healthy cluster of grapes means you are in the midst of abundance, lacking for nothing in the way of material goods. A grape with seeds indicates fertility; a seedless grape is a sign of a fruitless enterprise. If you peel grapes in a dream, you may want to get beneath the surface of another person, or become intimate with them.

Hair is a sign of sensuality, female beauty, and vanity. It is also is a sign for covering nakedness, and a symbol of submission. If you dream of long hair, you are concealing something you do not wish to show; if your hair is being cut, you fear loss of beauty or youth. White and grey hair symbolize the wisdom that comes with age, but may also indicate a fear of growing older. For men, hair is a sign of strength and virility, and baldness indicates a loss of power.

See *body*.

64

Horse

According to Jung, wild animals stand for our hidden emotions. The horse is a symbol of raw power and grace; a wild horse symbolizes freedom not possible within the constraints of everyday life. Horses are also signs of nobility, power, and prestige. A journey by horse relates also to your journey in life. Consider how the horse handles, what direction you are going, and whether you or the horse is in control. For instance, if you are riding a horse and can't keep your seat, you feel out of control in some aspect of your waking life.

See *airplane, bicycle, car, road*.

House

The house represents your psyche, and especially personal growth and expansion. If you are in a house you have known, you are exploring familiar regions of your own mind. If it is new, you are branching out in fresh directions. The parts of the house represent different parts of the self; the basement holds your deep, hidden emotions; the attic, your intellect. Long hallways, rooms with interesting shapes, and hidden passageways reflect the complexity and intrigue of your inner person; when you explore new passageways, you are experiencing growth and newness. A house with many rooms indicates you have many choices; a house with few rooms means your choices are few.

See *staircase, window*.

Jewelry

Jewels are a public display of money and prestige, and also indicate rarity and beauty. If you are wearing an over-abundance of jewelry, you are concerned with how you appear to others, and place emphasis on material values. For women, jewels represent love; for men, they are a sign of wealth. A diamond is a symbol of marriage, and may be related to issues of trust and commitment. A rare jewel may also represent your most valued possession.

See *crown, pearl*.

Kangaroo

With their powerful legs and keen sense of personal territory, kangaroos represent power that connot be easily controlled. In dreams, they point to areas in which you feel a continual need to assert yourself. If you are taking care of a feisty kangaroo, you may be experiencing difficulty with somebody who falls under your supervision. As marsupials, kangaroos represent the mother figure. Their young are particulary vulnerable to unfavorable environmental conditions and require utmost protection. A dream involving a kangaroo may signify unresolved issues regarding your mother's care for you, or point to your own maternal instincts.

Key

A key functions to open what is locked; coming into possession of a key indicates the possibility of entering

hidden spaces and discovering new worlds. It is a symbol of potential and intrigue, and carries with it adventure

and mystery. It is also a symbol of privilege: when you hold a key you have been granted access to a private place.

The key also functions as a sexual symbol—the lock symbolizes female sexuality, and the key, male sexuality.

Dreams of kissing are very often wish-fulfillment or compensation, especially if you are not in a position to receive physical affirmation in waking life. Consider whom you are kissing—if it is a stranger, you feel a need to conquer. If you kiss someone you know, you may harbor feelings for him or her. Watching people you know kiss is a sign that you know too much about their relationship and need distance.

Knot

A knot symbolizes a problem; the bigger the tangle, the more complicated the issue at hand. If you dream of a ball of string with one continuous tangle, problem solving may be tricky, but it is straightforward. String that branches off in different directions symbolizes tangental problems, and may be a bit more difficult to unwind. Consider whether the rope is used for a specific purpose. If possible, try to untie the knot. It could be your first step in resolving a complex problem in waking life.

Marriage

Dreams of marriage are very often fulfillment of your deep desires, especially if you are at a maturity level to take such a life-changing step. Conversely, marriage has to do with issues of fear and anxiety surrounding commitment. If you know the person you are meeting at the altar, consider what role he or she plays in your waking life. On a non-relational level, your unconscious may be urging you to continue on your path of self-realization.

Mirror

The mirror represents a vain, superficial image of the self. If you see yourself in a mirror you are concerned with perception, both how you see yourself and how others see you. A distorted mirror indicates that you have a false view of yourself. If you see yourself as heavier in a mirror than you are in real life, you desire to lose weight, or fear you are gaining weight. Conversely, the mirror can also symbolize the parts of yourself that are not readily seen, including your wishes and dreams. Consider what is different in the mirror than in the landscape of the dream.

Moon

The moon is a classic symbol of female energy, a sign of intuition, psychic power, and non-rational behavior. Just as the moon controls the earth's tides, it stands for loss of control due to changes in nature. A waxing moon indicates your intuition is ripening; a waning moon means you are becoming more rational and less intuitive. A full moon is a sign of completeness and wholeness.

Mother

The mother is a symbol of the unconscious and of intuitive, beneath-the-surface wisdom. Mother-figures often carry very personal meaning. If you dream of your own mother, you may be confronting issues in your past, or need to resolve issues at home. Dreaming of yourself as maternal means you are considering your relationship to a project of your own creation, or to family members or close relations whom you nurture emotionally. Traditionally, the woman is a sign for the emotive side of the self.

See *old man, old woman*.

Mountain

Mountains are signs of personal challenge and motivation. If you reach the top of a steep slope to emerge on a mountaintop, you are achieving your goals and have reason to feel proud of your personal success. Ascent means you are going towards a goal; descent means you have attained an objective and are now venturing to a place of less pressure. It may also indicate a loss of life goals, or the disappointment that comes after success as you find you have less to reach for. If you come to an impasse, there is something blocking your way in waking life. If you find a way around the obstacle in your dream, you may become "unblocked" in your real life.

Nudity

Dreaming you are naked in a public setting is very common, and often relates to feelings of unwanted exposure and vulnerability. In particular, it relates to fear that others won't accept the "true" self hidden beneath your exterior.

Conversely, if you are not concerned with modesty, the dream may be one of freedom from or rebellion against society's norms. If only one part of you is unclothed, consider what it means to be exposed in that particular area.

If others don't notice your nakedness until you do, you are harboring secrets you'd rather not reveal.

Old Man, Old Woman

The wise old woman and man are archetypes, universal symbols that may be found in many dream settings. Both symbolize wisdom, maturity, and access to the spiritual realm, but may conversely lead you away from a higher state of consciousness. Pay close attention to anything the old man or woman imparts to you; its meaning can usually be read in a much larger scope than your personal life. The old woman or man can be found in such figures as priests, teachers, magicians, doctors, or persons of venerable age.

Pearls

A pearl represents a thing of great worth, not to be parted with at any cost. If you dream of finding a pearl, you value the rare and the beautiful. If you are cultivating pearls, you understand the patience needed to build and maintain a personal fortune. Pearls also represent "becoming"—they begin as tiny grains of sand in an oyster shell, and only after years of incubation, become prized objects. Finding a pearl also means you are gifted at finding treasure among ordinary objects.

See *jewelry, crown*.

Prison

A locked cell is symbolic of any kind of entrapment you find yourself in, whether by circumstance, emotion, or life choices. Being kept from free movement implies a loss of power or choice; perhaps you have been unable to grow in your personal or professional life. Conversely, being held in jail may mean you feel ashamed for some action or feeling, and are being "punished" by your inner self. Consider who your captors are. If you are the captor, you would like to assert control over another person.

Road

Travel indicates you are dealing with where you are going in life, whether it has to do with long-term direction or everyday goals. Several factors are important in interpreting this dream symbol fully: the condition of the road or path, how straight or curvy it is, the surrounding scenery, your companions, other people or vehicles on the road. Are you on a one-lane dirt road, a barely discernable footpath, a four-lane highway? Are you walking, or is something carrying you? What obstacles are in your path, and how do you navigate around them?

See *airplane, bicycle, car.*

Like all flowers, roses in dreams symbolize natural beauty and the feminine. Above all other flowers, roses are symbols of romance, especially if they are deep red. A white rose is a sign of innocence and purity; a black rose symbolizes the death of love. Thorns are obstacles on the path to intimacy. Consider where the roses came from, whether they were given to you by another, found in the wild, or given by you to someone. A blossoming rose symbolizes young love; a wilting rose signifies loss of love, or loss of youth.

Running

As a purely physical act, the sensation of running symbolizes progress and productivity. Consider your destination, and where you are coming from. If you are running from someone, you are vulnerable to personal attack, or fearful something outside of your control will cause you harm. If, as often happens in dreams, you are unable to run away from your pursuers, you are "caught" in some area of your life and frozen from action by a fear of confronting the real issue. Learning more about lucid dreaming may "free" you. Conversely, you fear being caught for something you have done. Consider whether you fit the role of victim or perpetrator.

Sand

Sand is a sign of instability and things temporary or fleeting. Like the biblical parable reminds us, sand is not a good foundation for building—it causes structural weakness and possible collapse. Dreaming of sand may mean you have central instability you would not like to admit, but it could lead to a fall. If you dream you are running your fingers through sand, you are concerned that time is slipping by too quickly. Smooth sand upon the beach is a renewing symbol, as the cycle of tides makes it smooth each day.

School

School dreams are very often related to anxiety, and depend greatly upon your own experiences with it. If you driven to succeed, you may be concerned about "making the grade" in your present life or job situation. If you were often in trouble, you are concerned that you will be called on recent behavior. If you were shy or had trouble keeping up, you may be reliving some of your pent-up emotions, or dealing with similar issues today. Common scenarios in school dreams include being called upon to recite from memory, being unprepared for class, coming to school not fully dressed, failing a test, or having to complete requirements for a degree already completed.

Skeleton

The skeleton symbolizes a fear of death, or a fear of having the past sneak up on you. Culturally, the "skeleton in the closet" may appear as the personification of a deep, hidden secret, often one that has to do with family. To dream you are burying a set of bones means you are leaving the past behind. Bones are also significant—they are the body's foundation, strength, and what gives us our frame. Weak or broken bones indicate a character flaw or confusion about identity.

See *body*.

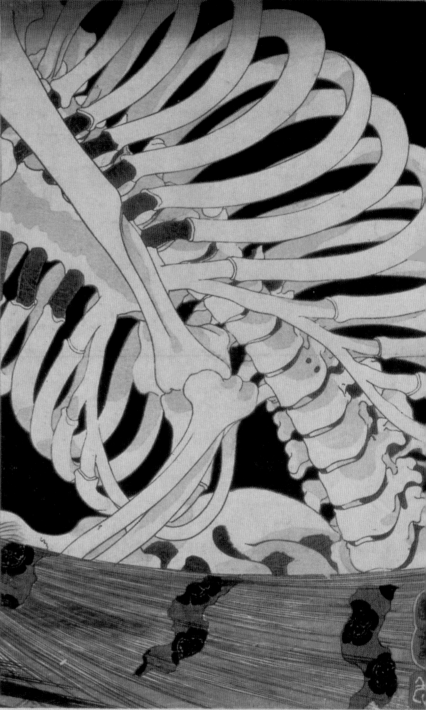

The sky symbolizes transcendence and the truths we take for granted. Even when the sky is filled with clouds, you trust there is blue sky behind them. To dream of the sky means you are looking for constancy or stability. A blue sky means the future is limitless; a cloudy sky is a sign of worry, unease, and obstacles to success. You may also find meaning in the shape of the clouds.

See *storm*.

Sleeping

Falling asleep is a common dream experience, often a sign of lucid or controlled dreaming. If you fall asleep within the course of a dream, you are in touch with your unconscious self. A dream within a dream is a direct line to your unconscious, and may be read quite literally. The bedroom is a place of intimate relationships, and a symbol of the places you keep private. Consider whether you are alone or with another person.

See *bed.*

Snake

The snake is a many-headed dream symbol. In one analysis, the snake that sheds its skin is a sign of growth and renewal, of transition and change. Consider what it is you are leaving behind. In cultural analysis, the serpent is the symbol of temptation, seduction, and misplaced loyalty, synonymous with evil and the devil. Being afraid of a snake in a dream may also relate to a fear of male sexuality, and, like all wild animals, stands for hidden emotion.

See *devil*.

Staircase

The staircase is a symbol for movement within the psyche, especially in terms of personal growth. To go up suggests a journey into the spiritual or intellectual part of yourself, while a downward direction indicates you are traveling into your unconscious. Individual steps may be read as stages of personal growth. A spiral staircase indicates a journey that is spiritual in nature. See *house*.

Storm

Storms are symbols of very strong emotional reaction to an outside event. A sudden storm implies emotional uproar, especially if you are already experiencing a great amount of change in your waking life. They also express fear that you cannot maintain emotional stability. Storms arise in dreams for many reasons, such as unforeseen family problems, unexpected loss, or long spiritual battle. Thunder is a sign of the tearing loose of repressed emotions. A tornado or hurricane is a sign of impending, possibly devastating personal crisis. See *sky*.

Tree

The tree is a sign of fertility and family heritage. If you dream of a new tree sprouting, you see the potential of a new relationship or project, or potential within your own family for growth. You may have a desire to see your family expand. If you dream of a great tree, you are visualizing your own family history; the roots are the past and the green leaves, the present generation. The tree is also a sign for the Christian cross, and symbolizes the triumph of life over death.

See *apple*.

Violin

The violin is a symbol of romance and beauty. If you hear stringed music in a dream, you are being swept away by feelings of love. Hearing music also indicates your own creativity and keen sense of enjoyment for a skill that is hard-earned. If you dream you play the violin, you long to have the ability to pick up what is difficult and make it look easy.

Water

Water is a symbol of cleansing and purification. The state of the water is indicative of your emotional state. Muddy water is a sign of confusion; fast-flowing water means you do not wish to be towed under by circumstance, or are excited about new prospects. Warm water is an invitation; cold indicates refusal. Water also acts as a gauge for your love life; the bigger the body of water in your dream, the more "in love" you feel, whether it is the size of a small mountain stream or vast ocean.

Window

Windows are metaphors of our attitude towards the outside world. A closed window indicates isolation; an open window, optimism and friendship. If the glass is dirty, you may have difficulty seeing the world from any perspective other than your own. Looking into someone else's window is a sign of curiosity that borders on voyeurism—perhaps you need to distance yourself. If you break a window, you've done something to disrupt a situation and aren't sure how to put the pieces back together again.

See *house*.

Credits

Front cover and pp. 84–85: *Moon Maiden* (2000), by Roxana Villa. Courtesy of the artist, www.RoxanaVilla.com.

Back cover and p. 13: *Apples and Oranges* (1895–1900), by Paul Cezanne. Musée d'Orsay, Paris, France; Lauros-Giraudon-Bridgeman Art Library.

p. 9: *Hope over Cuba*, by unknown Cuban artist. Private Collection; The Art Archive/Mireille Vautier.

p. 10: *Angel*, portal of Basilica of Saint Angelo (11th century), artist unknown. Museo di Capodimonte, Naples; The Art Archive/Dagli Orti.

p. 14: *The Young Mother*, by Mary Cassatt. Private Collection; Christie's Images/Bridgeman Art Library.

pp. 16–17: *Kamei Rokuro and the Black Bear in the Snow* (1849), by Kuniyoshi Utagawa. Private Collection; Bridgeman Art Library.

p. 18: *Le Lit (The Bed)* (c. 1892), by Henri de Toulouse-Lautrec. Musée d'Orsay, Paris; The Art Archive/Dagli Orti.

p. 21: *Cycling Race* (1902), by George Duchesne. Musée de la Voiture, Compiegne, France; Réunion des Musées Nationaux/Art Resource, New York.

p. 22: *The Blind Girl* (1856), by Sir John Everett Millais. Birmingham Museums and Art Gallery; Bridgeman Art Library.

p. 25: *Study of a Nude Young Man Sitting* (c. 1836), by Hippolyte Flandrin. Louvre, Paris, France; Réunion des Musées Nationaux/Art Resource, New York.

p. 26: *Harmond* (2001) by Christina Hess. Courtesy of the artist.

p. 29: *Waterlily Pond* (1899), by Claude Monet. National Gallery, London, UK/Bridgeman Art Library.

p. 30: *Etruscan family sarcophagus*. Cerveteri (Caere), Tuscany, Italy; Bridgeman Art Library.

p. 33: *The Road with Acacias* (1908), by Roger de La Fresnaye. Musee de la Ville de Paris, Musee Carnavalet, Paris; France/Lauros-Giraudon-Bridgeman Art Library.

p. 34: *Cat Woman* (1990), by Mahvash Mossaed. Courtesy of the artist, www.mahvashmossaed.com.

p. 37: *Emperor Otto IV Playing Chess with Woman. . .* (1381). University Library Heidelberg; The Art Archive/Dagli Orti.

p. 38: *Boy in a Sailor Suit*, by Amedeo Modigliani. The Barnes Foundation, Merion, Pennsylvania, USA; Bridgeman Art Library.

p. 41: *Le Cirque (The Circus)* (1890–91), by Georges Seurat. Musée d'Orsay, Paris, France; Erich Lessing/Art Resource, New York.

p. 42: *Radiance* (1999), by Roxana Villa. Courtesy of the artist, www.RoxanaVilla.com.

p. 45: *Q is for Queen* (2000), by Rachel Bliss. Courtesy of the artist.

p. 46: *After My Death* (1999), by Mahvash Mossaed. Courtesy of the artist, www.mahvashmossaed.com.

p. 49: *The Devil Taking a Child* (14th century), by Francesco Melanzio. Pinacoteca-Museo Comunale, Montefalco, Italy; The Art Archive/Dagli Orti.

p. 50: *A Composite Elephant with Buddhist Deities and Figures Attached to Trunk*, from *Elephant Treatise* (1850) by Thai artist. British Library; The Art Archive/British Library.

p. 53: *Hide Me in Your Pocket* (1991), by Mahvash Mossaed. Courtesy of the artist, www.mahvashmossaed.com.

p. 54: *February, Man Warming Himself*, folio 58R, *Breviary of Love* (13th century), by Ermengol de Beziers. Real Biblioteca de lo Escorial; The Art Archive/Dagli Orti.

p. 57: *The Promenade* (1917), by Marc Chagall. Russian State Museum, St. Petersburg, Russia; Scala/Art Resource, New York. © 2002 Artists Rights Society (ARS), New York/ADAGP, Paris.

p. 58: *The Luncheon of the Boating Party* (1881), by Pierre Auguste Renoir. Phillips Collection, Washington, DC, USA; Bridgeman Art Library.

p. 60: *The Three Kings*, Armenian manuscript detail (1392), by Youhannès de Berkri. Armenian Museum Isfahan; The Art Archive/Dagli Orti.

p. 63: *Picking Grapes*, fresco from tomb of Nakht. Valley of the Nobles, Qurna, Thebes, Egypt; The Art Archive/Dagli Orti.

p. 65: *Woman Drying Herself* (1894), by Edgar Degas. Tate Gallery, London, UK; The Art Archive/Album/Joseph Martin.

p. 66: *Emerging* (1995), by Helen Mirkil. Courtesy of the artist.

p. 69: *House and Figure* (1890), by Vincent van Gogh. The Barnes Foundation, Merion, Pennsylvania, USA; Bridgeman Art Library.

p. 70: *Empress Theodora* (500–548 AD). Mosaic from Basilica San Vitale, Ravenna, Italy; The Art Archive/Dagli Orti.

pp. 72–73: *Kangaroo and Dingo*, by Irvala. Musée des Arts Africains et Océaniens; The Art Archive/Dagli Orti.

p. 74: *Saint Peter* (12th century). Monte Maria Abbey, Burgusio, Bolzano, Italy; The Art Archive/Dagli Orti.

p. 77: *The Kiss* (1907–08), by Gustav Klimt. Osterreichische Galerie, Vienna, Austria; Bridgeman Art Library.

p. 78: *The Knot of Solomon* (4th century). Basilica Aquileia, Italy; The Art Archive/Dagli Orti.

p. 81: *The Artist and His Wife,* or *The Young Married Couple* (1980), by Marc Chagall. Pushkin Museum, Moscow, Russia; Bridgeman Art Library. © 2002 Artists Rights Society (ARS), New York/ADAGP, Paris.

p. 83: *The Discovery* (1993), by Mahvash Mossaed. Courtesy of the artist, www.mahvashmossaed.com.

p. 86: *Mother and Child* (c. 1904), by Paula Modersohn-Becker. Haags Gemeentemuseum, Netherlands; Bridgeman Art Library.

p. 89: *La Ceida* (1993), by Diana Kan. © Diana Kan/Licensed by VAGA, New York, NY. Photography by Sing-Si Schwartz.

p. 90: *Female Nude* (c. 1916), by Amedeo Modigliani. Courtauld Institute Gallery, Somerset House, London, UK; Bridgeman Art Library.

p. 93: *Portrait of an Old Man*, attributed to Theodore Gericault. Christie's Images, London, UK; Bridgeman Art Library.

p. 94: *Battista Sforza, Wife of Federico da Montefeltro* (c. 1465), by Francesca della Piero. Galleria degli Uffizi, Florence, Italy; The Art Archive/Dagli Orti.

p. 97: *The Exercise Yard,* or *The Convict Prison* (1890), by Vincent van Gogh. Pushkin Museum, Moscow, Russia; Bridgeman Art Library.

p. 98: *Daily Life Scene in Village in Haiti*, possibly by Julio Buairi. Georges Heraux Collection, Port au Prince, Haiti; The Art Archive/Mireille Vautier.

p. 101: *Summer Offering* (1911), by Sir Lawrence Alma-Tadema. Private Collection; Bridgeman Art Library.

p. 102: *Two Women Running on the Beach,* or *The Race* (1922), by Pablo Picasso. Musee Picasso, Paris, France; Peter Willi/Bridgeman Art Library. © 2002 Estate of Pablo Picasso/Artists Rights Society (ARS), New York.

p. 105: *Summer Evening on the Skagen Southern Beach with Anna Ancher and Marie Kroyer* (1893), by Peder Severin Kroyer. Skagens Museum, Denmark; Bridgeman Art Library.

p. 106: *The Dictation* (1891), by D. Cassola. Galleria d'Arte Moderna, Turin, Italy; Alinari/Art Resource, New York.

pp. 108–109: *Mitsukini Defying the Skeleton Spectre* (c. 1845), by Kuniyoshi Utagawa. Victoria & Albert Museum, London, UK; Bridgeman Art Library.

p. 110: *Horse Path* (2000), by Helen Mirkil. Collection of Langhorne Smith.

p. 112: *Flaming June* (c. 1895), by Frederic Leighton. Museo de Arte, Ponce, Puerto Rico, West Indies; Bridgeman Art Library.

p. 115: *Eve* (c. 1906–07), by Henri J.F. Rousseau. Hamburg Kunsthalle, Hamburg, Germany; Bridgeman Art Library.

p. 117: *Jacob's Ladder* (c. 1800), by William Blake. British Museum, London, UK; Bridgeman Art Library.

p. 118: *Night of Jealousy* (1893), by Johan August Strindberg. Strindberg Museum, Stockholm, Sweden; The Art Archive/Dagli Orti.

p. 121: *Untitled* (1998) by Kelly Stribling Sutherland. Courtesy of the artist and www.friendandjohnson.com.

p. 122: *Still Life with a Violin* (1921), by Kuzma Sergeevich Petrov-Vodkin. Private Collection; Bridgeman Art Library.

p. 125: *Awa Province Naruto Rapids* (1855), by Ando Hiroshige. Victoria & Albert Museum, London, UK; The Art Archive/Sally Chappell.

p. 126: *Interior on the Isle of Wight* (1875), by Berthe Morisot. Private Collection, Paris; Giruadon/Art Resource, New York.